BISON
BOOKS

HERMAN J. VIOLA

WITH JAN SHELTON DANIS

IT IS A GOOD DAY TO DIE

Indian Eyewitnesses
Tell the Story
of the
Battle of the Little Bighorn

UNIVERSITY OF NEBRASKA PRESS
LINCOLN AND LONDON

(∞)

First Bison Books printing: 2001
Photographic acknowledgments can be found on page 101.

Library of Congress Cataloging-in-Publication Data
Viola, Herman J.
It is a good day to die: Indian eyewitnesses tell the story of the Battle of the Little
Bighorn / Herman J. Viola with Jan Shelton Danis.
p.   cm.
Originally published: New York: Crown, c1998.
Includes bibliographical references and index.
ISBN 0-8032-9626-6 (pbk.: alk. paper)
1. Little Bighorn, Battle of the, Mont., 1876—Personal narratives.   2. Dakota Indi-
ans—Wars, 1876.   3. Cheyenne Indians—Wars, 1876.   4. Custer, George Armstrong,
1839–1876.   I. Danis, Jan Shelton.   II. Title.
E83.876 .V56   2001
973.8'2—dc21   2001034669

Contents

IT IS A
GOOD DAY
TO DIE

Author's Note

The Sioux were once one of the largest tribes in North America. The name "Sioux" derives from an Ojibwe word which means "snake" or "enemy." The tribe prefers to be known by the word for themselves as spoken in the three main dialects of the Siouan language, namely Lakota, Dakota, and Nakota, which means "allies." Most of the tribal members who participated in the Battle of the Little Big Horn were Lakotas. Their Eastern relatives in Minnesota, popularly known as the Santee Sioux, are Dakotas. I have therefore used the term Lakota or Dakota except in Indian accounts of the battle, where the tribal names remain as originally recorded by the historians who interviewed the individuals whose accounts appear here.

Introduction

I am an old man, and soon my spirit must leave this earth to join the spirits of my fathers. Therefore, I shall speak only the truth in telling what I know of the fight on the Little Horn River where General Custer was killed. Curly, who was with us, will tell you that I do not lie.

This is how White Man Runs Him, a member of the Crow Indian tribe, replied to questions about his part in the famous battle known to generations of white Americans as "Custer's Last Stand." He had been a young warrior, only about eighteen years old, when he agreed to help the U.S. Army find and fight the Lakota and Cheyennes, who were bitter enemies of his Crow people. With White Man Runs Him were five other Crow warriors serving as scouts for Custer's Seventh Cavalry. Curly was one of them. They survived the battle, but Custer and more than 250 troopers did not. Fought on June 25, 1876, the Battle of the Little Bighorn River—or the "Greasy Grass," as it was known to the Lakota Indians—was a dramatic victory for the Lakota and Cheyenne peoples over the U.S. government.

In their old age, the former scouts and Lakota and Cheyenne veterans of the battle were often questioned by reporters, historians, and other individuals curious to know exactly what had taken place at the battle. How was it that the Indians, whom most whites believed to be undisciplined and poorly armed, were able to defeat one of the finest fighting forces in the U.S. Army? Was it poor leadership by Custer? Was it widespread panic and fear by inexperienced soldiers? Was it the clever generalship of Sitting Bull, who lured Custer into an elaborate trap? Or was it the Everywhere Spirit, fulfilling a prediction made to Sitting Bull, who had had a vision during the Sun Dance of soldiers falling upside down into his village?

The Northern Cheyennes still believe the victory was due to Custer's failure to keep a promise made almost a decade earlier to their kinsmen, the Southern Cheyennes of Oklahoma. In 1869, after fighting and defeating the Southern Cheyennes, Custer smoked a pipe of peace with Cheyenne leaders. As part of the ceremony, Custer made a promise never to make war on the Cheyennes again. The Cheyenne chiefs warned him that if he failed to listen carefully to their words and failed to keep this solemn vow, great harm would befall him. That is why, after his body was found and recognized on the battlefield, two Cheyenne women punctured his ears with their sewing awls. They did this to help him hear better in the afterlife—because he had obviously failed to hear, or heed, the warning their chiefs had made in 1869.

At first, Indian veterans of the battle refused to tell their stories out of fear of punishment by the U.S. government. Even today, some descendants of the Lakota and Cheyennes who fought that day are reluctant to tell outsiders the stories about the battle that they heard from their parents and grandparents. Even when Indians talked about the battle, army investigators and historians tended to discredit their accounts, believing that they were somehow trying to conceal the truth. Now, after the passage of so many years, this attitude has changed. The Indians' stories are acknowledged as providing a vivid picture of events that day. And because none of the soldiers with Custer lived to tell what happened, theirs is the only account that survives.

The followers of Sitting Bull, Gall, and Crazy Horse fought as individuals, not as members of military units like a troop of cavalry, and their stories are individual versions of events. Because the Indian village was caught by surprise, there was no overall battle plan. Each woman, child, and warrior had only a personal perspective of the battle. It requires the comparison of many individual stories to obtain some idea of what happened. In truth, there was a great deal of confusion. Clouds of dust thrown up by galloping horses and the black smoke from hundreds of gunshots obscured everything. At the height of the battle it was hard to tell Indian from white man. Therefore, no precise accounting of what happened during the battle will ever be possible.

Most of the individuals who appear in this book told their stories many years after the battle. Even in their old age, however, they had vivid memories of that June day in 1876 when Custer and the Seventh Cavalry surprised the followers of Sitting Bull in their camp along the banks of the Greasy Grass.

The trail to the Greasy Grass began in the 1840s, when the first white settlers started crossing the Great Plains in their covered wagons, seeking homes in the fertile valleys of California and Oregon. The small trickle of settlers eventually became a torrent, thanks to the construction of railroads and government initiatives such as the 1862 Homestead Act, which gave land free to homesteaders.

As the flow of settlers increased, Indians across the West tried to defend their land and their way of life. Among the Dakota people of the northern Great Plains, the Santee, who lived in present-day Minnesota, fought an unsuccessful campaign against settlers and the U.S. Army in 1862. Defeated by the superior firepower and numbers of the army, some of the Santee fled west to join Lakota bands living in the Dakota Territory.

More successful was Red Cloud, a leader of the Oglala, whose two-year fight against the U.S. Army forced the

Red Cloud.

government to abandon forts built along the Bozeman Trail, which ran through Lakota hunting grounds in what is now eastern Montana and Wyoming. At Fort Laramie, Wyoming, in 1868, Red Cloud and other Lakota leaders signed a treaty that temporarily ended hostilities on the northern plains and created the Great Sioux Reservation, in what is now South Dakota, west of the Missouri River. The

Treaty negotiations at Fort Laramie, Wyoming, April 1868.

Black Hills Expedition, 1874.

treaty also gave the Lakota permission to continue to use their traditional hunting grounds as long as the buffalo and other game animals were plentiful enough to feed them. However, the chiefs who signed the treaty—including Red Cloud—agreed to one day accept life on reservations, where they would receive food, clothes, money, cattle, and farm supplies from government officials called Indian agents. On the reservations, teachers, missionaries, and farmers would instruct the Indians in a new way of life.

Sitting Bull, leader of the Hunkpapa band of the Lakota,

did not sign the Treaty of Fort Laramie. He and other leaders, such as Crazy Horse, instead chose the life of their fathers, moving their villages from place to place and hunting the buffalo. "I am a red man," Sitting Bull proclaimed. "If the Great Spirit had desired me to be a white man, he would have made me so in the first place. It is not necessary for eagles to be crows. Now we are poor, but we are free. I do not wish to be shut up in a corral. All reservation Indians I have seen are worthless. They are neither red warriors nor white farmers. They are neither wolf nor dog."

Soon after the Fort Laramie Treaty was signed, white settlers began to press closer to the Great Sioux Reservation. The once-unlimited buffalo herds, upon which the Plains Indians depended for their livelihood, became harder and harder to find. Surveyors began illegally mapping railroad routes across Indian land, including the Great Sioux Reservation. Then, in 1874, the government sent a scientific expedition into the Black Hills, an area to the west of the Great Sioux Reservation that was—and is to this day—sacred to the Lakota and Cheyenne Indians. The expedition, which was led by Lieutenant Colonel George Armstrong Custer, found

George Armstrong Custer (seated), photographed during an 1874 expedition to protect surveyors of the Northern Pacific Railroad. To Custer's right is the Arikara scout Bloody Knife.

gold in the Black Hills. Prospectors soon overran the region, and the army faced a losing struggle trying to keep them off Indian land. After an effort to buy the Black Hills failed, the government accused Sitting Bull, Crazy Horse, Gall, and the independent Lakota bands of having violated the Treaty of Fort Laramie. Late in 1875, the government sent messengers to all the free-roaming bands: "Come to the reservation or be considered hostiles against whom the United States Army will make war."

When the deadline of January 31, 1876, passed and the Indians did not come onto the reservations, the U.S. Army made good the threat. Between March and May 1876, it sent three columns of soldiers to Montana under General George

Crook, Colonel John Gibbon, and General Alfred Terry. Their orders were to find the Indians and force them onto the Great Sioux Reservation. In March 1876, after Crook attacked a Cheyenne camp on the Powder River, Lakota and Cheyenne bands began camping together for mutual protection from the soldiers. Their strength was further increased by warriors from the reservation—young men who heard that Sitting Bull wanted to drive the white men from the Black Hills and who were eager to earn honors in battle.

The Indians were not anxious to fight, but neither were

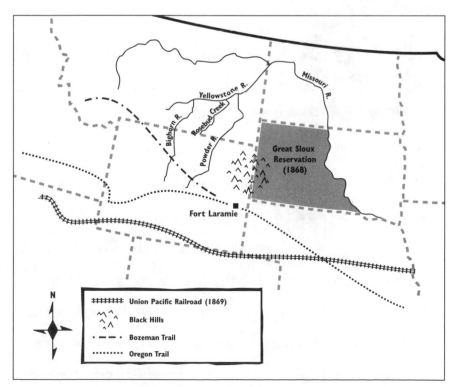

they afraid of the soldiers. They were well armed. Indeed, many of them carried better rifles than those issued to the army. The Indians were also proud, defiant, and superbly led by the charismatic Sitting Bull and the brilliant war chief Crazy Horse. Other important chiefs were Gall and Hump of the Lakota and Dull Knife, Lame White Man, and Two Moon of the Cheyennes. Their confidence was bolstered by a vision Sitting Bull had while undergoing the Sun Dance, in which

he saw many dead soldiers "falling right into our camp."

On June 17, scouts brought word to Crazy Horse that soldiers were marching toward their camp along the nearby Rosebud Creek. Crazy Horse met them with a large force of Lakota and Cheyenne warriors. The Battle of the Rosebud lasted

Sitting Bull.

six hours and ended only after the Indians got tired of fighting. What saved Crook's infantry from disaster was the vigilance and bravery of his Indian allies—Shoshone and Crow scouts whose skilled horsemanship stopped a Lakota and Cheyenne surprise attack and kept them at bay while the soldiers got into battle formation.

Meanwhile, Gibbon and Terry, unaware of Crook's defeat, met on the Yellowstone River at the mouth of the Rosebud. Terry sent some six hundred cavalry under Lieutenant Colonel Custer to follow a fresh Indian trail leading to the Bighorn River. With Custer were six Crow and forty Arikara scouts. Custer's orders were to locate the village and wait for reinforcements. Meanwhile, the infantry with Gibbon and Terry would follow as quickly as possible and then attack the village from at least two directions so the Indians would be unable to escape.

The Crow and Arikara scouts easily found the village, but warned Custer that there were too many warriors in it and that his tired cavalry should not risk an attack. They urged him to wait for the expected reinforcements.

The village was indeed huge. It held some twelve hundred tepees in six large tribal circles. Five circles belonged to Lakota tribal bands—Hunkpapa, Oglala, Miniconjou, Sans Arc, Blackfeet—and one was Northern Cheyenne. The village stretched along the Greasy Grass for approximately three miles. In the village were upward of ten thousand people, including as many as two thousand fighting men. The horse herd was gigantic—twenty-five thousand head.

Custer feared that the Indians would slip away if he waited for Gibbon and Terry, so despite his scouts' warnings, he decided to attack at once. At noon on June 25, he divided his force into three units, leaving a few troopers to guard the mule train laden with supplies and extra ammunition. One unit, under Captain Frederick Benteen, was sent to cut off the escape of Indians to the left of the village. A second unit, under Major Marcus Reno, was ordered to attack the village directly. Custer's unit swung around to the right of the village, expecting to attack it from another direction while the Indians were occupied with Reno. The key to Custer's strategy appears to have been the expectation that most of the Indians in the village would run away rather than fight.

Reno charged the village as ordered, but the warriors did not run away. Instead, they rushed forward, in order to give their families time to get out of the village and seek refuge in the nearby hills. As a result, Reno's troopers quickly found themselves confronted by hundreds of angry warriors led by Chief Gall of the Hunkpapa. Gall was the adopted brother of Sitting Bull and an able war chief. During Reno's attack,

Gall's two wives and three children were killed because their tent was close to the scene of the fighting.

The Indians stopped Reno's attack and then began to surround his outnumbered troopers, forcing them to make a hasty and disorderly dash to some bluffs along the river. Reno lost a third of his men during the retreat, although some managed to hide in bushes along the river and later rejoined their comrades under cover of darkness.

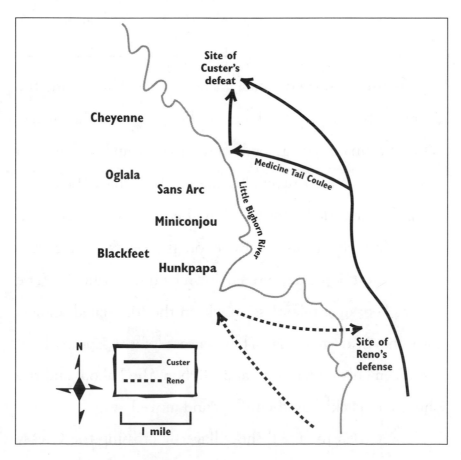

Custer's last note, written to Captain Benteen: "Come on. Big village. Be quick. Bring packs."

Custer continued out of sight behind the bluffs along the river with the idea of attacking another portion of the village. When he finally got a good view of the camp, he sent an urgent message to Benteen: "Come on. Big village. Be quick. Bring [ammunition] packs." But Benteen never reached Custer. Instead, he joined Reno on the bluffs, where they spent the rest of the day pinned down by Indian rifle fire. The Indians kept up a relentless attack on the frightened soldiers until the next morning. Then, aware of the approach of reinforcements under Terry and Gibbon, the Lakota and the Cheyennes packed up their tents and moved away.

Custer tried to attack the village by crossing the Greasy

Grass at Medicine Tail Coulee, which provided a path for horsemen midway into the village, but Indian sharpshooters forced the soldiers back. Custer and his officers then had the troops form a large, uneven defensive square while they waited for the reinforcements that never came. Meanwhile, seeing that Benteen and Reno were content to remain on the bluffs, most of the warriors at that front rushed back to confront Custer.

A warrior who played a key role in the destruction of Custer's command was Crazy Horse, one of the most respected and revered of the Lakota leaders. In battle his hair flowed freely, with a single eagle feather hanging tip down. His face

A painting by the Lakota artist Amos Bad Heart Bull shows Crazy Horse charging Custer's cavalry during the Battle of the Little Bighorn. Crazy Horse refused to allow his photograph to be taken, and no likeness of him exists.

paint was a red zigzag line with white spots that symbolized the lightning and hail of the thunder spirits. Crazy Horse's medicine—his spiritual power—was so strong that it was believed no bullet could touch him. At a critical moment in the battle, mounted on his buckskin pinto and blowing an eagle-bone whistle, he dashed back and forth across a line of Custer's dismounted troops, daring them to shoot him. Each time he rode past, the soldiers fired and missed with their single-shot carbines. "I will pass before them a third time," Crazy Horse yelled to his followers, who were shielded by thick sagebrush. "As soon as they shoot their guns, rush forward before they have time to reload."

Inspired by Crazy Horse's bravery, the hidden Indians dashed forward. Many of Custer's soldiers panicked and began to run toward the center of the defensive square. The troopers melted away as the Lakota and Cheyennes rushed among them, hitting them with clubs and tomahawks. One of the Lakota veterans later remarked, "It was like hunting buffalo."

"It Is a Good Day to Die"

Sitting Bull
Hunkpapa

I never taught my people to trust the Americans. I told them the truth—the Americans are great liars. I have never dealt with the Americans. I never went to the reservation or accepted rations or other gifts from the white man government. My people were wealthy in food and clothing and lodges, in everything necessary for being an Indian.

The land belonged to my people. It was a gift to us from the Great Spirit. The Great Spirit gave us the game in this country. It was our privilege to hunt the game in our country. The white man came here to take the country from us by force. He brought misery and wretchedness into our country. We were here killing game and eating, and all of a sudden we were attacked by white men. We were not out there to fight; we had to fight because we were attacked.

Low Dog
Oglala

At that time we Oglalas had no thought that we would ever fight the whites. Then I heard some people talking that the chief of the white men wanted the Indians to live where he ordered and do as he said, and he would feed and clothe them. I was called into council with the chiefs and wise men, and we had a talk about that. My judgment was, Why should I allow any man to support me against my will anywhere, so long as I have hands and so long as I am an able man, not a boy? Little I thought then that I would have to fight the white man, or do as he should tell me. When it began to be plain that we would have to yield or fight, we had a great many councils. I said, Why should I be kept as a humble man, when I am a brave warrior and on my own lands? The game is mine, and the hills, and the valleys, and the white man has no right to say where I shall go or what I shall do. If any white man tries to destroy what is mine, or take my lands, I will take my gun, get on my horse, and go punish him.

Antelope Woman
Cheyenne

The band of Cheyennes that I lived with had about forty family lodges. In the last part of the winter we camped on the west side of Powder River, not far above the mouth of Little Powder River. Soldiers came early one morning in March 1876. They got between our camp and our horse herds, so that all of us had to run away on foot. Not many of our people were killed, but our tepees and everything in them were burned. Three days later, all of us walking, we arrived at the camp of Crazy Horse, the Oglala Sioux chief.

The Oglalas gave us food and shelter. After a few days the two bands went northward and found the Hunkpapa Sioux, where Sitting Bull was chief. The leaders of the three tribes decided that all of us should travel together for the spring and summer hunting.

We moved from place to place as the grass came up. Because Indians kept coming from the Dakota reservation, our three bands grew larger and larger. Other tribal bands joined us. Miniconjou Sioux, Blackfeet Sioux, Arrows All Gone Sioux—all came with us. There were then six separate camp circles, each having its own chiefs, wherever we camped. In some of the other camps there were small bands of other Sioux—the Burned Thigh, the Assiniboine, and some Waist and Skirt people.

All of us traveled together to the west side of the lower Powder River, on west across the Tongue River, and then to the Rosebud valley where the grass was high and our ponies became strong. Our men killed many buffalo, and we women tanned the hides and dried the meat as we moved from place to place up the Rosebud.

Sitting Bull

Early summer is the season for Sun Dance among the Sioux people. I had pledged one hundred pieces of flesh to the Great Spirit, and I fulfilled my vow. My brother Jumping Bull cut tiny pieces of skin—fifty from each arm—using an awl and a sharp knife. I danced two days and two nights. God sent me a vision. I saw white soldiers and enemy Indians on horseback falling into the Sioux camp. They were coming down like grasshoppers, head first, with their hats falling off. Just then I heard a voice from above, saying, "I give you these because they have no ears!"

Black Moon was conducting the Sun Dance. He announced this vision to all who were present, all the Sioux and Cheyennes who were traveling together. We were camped on the Rosebud River at that time, three days before we defeated the white soldiers there and ten days before our victory on the Little Bighorn.

Wooden Leg
Cheyenne

In the summer of the great battle on the Little Bighorn, I was eighteen years old and among the tallest men of the tribe of Northern Cheyennes. Many young men were anxious to go for fighting the soldiers. But the chiefs and old men all urged us to keep away from the white men. They said that fighting wasted energy that ought to be applied in looking only for food and clothing, trying only to feed and make comfortable ourselves and our families. Our combination of camps was simply for defense. We were within our treaty rights as hunters. We must keep ourselves so.

We moved over to the Little Bighorn after we had beaten the white men soldiers at the fight on the Rosebud. Our scouts had followed them far enough to learn that they were going farther and farther away from us. We did not know of any other soldiers hunting for us. If there were any, they now would be afraid to come. There were feasts and dances in all of the camps. On the benchlands just east of us our horses found plenty of rich grass. Among the hills west of the river were great herds of buffalo. Every day, big hunting parties went among them. Men and women were at work providing for their families. That was why we killed these animals. Indians never did destroy any animal life as a mere pleasurable adventure.

Young Hawk

Arikara, a scout in Custer's cavalry unit

At Fort Abraham Lincoln in our country, General Custer told us that the Sioux bands had united and he was going on an expedition against them. About forty of us Arikaras decided to serve with him as scouts. A few days before the big battle, we were on the Rosebud River. The scouts were told to practice our death songs. The Sioux trail had been seen and the fight would soon be on.

We came to an abandoned Sioux camp where we found a Sun Dance circle. I saw in one of the sweat lodges, where they had camped, three stones near the middle, all in a row and painted red. To the Sioux this meant the Great Spirit would give them victory. Another scout, named Soldier, saw four sticks standing upright with a buffalo calfskin tied on with cloth and other articles of value. All the Arikaras knew this was evidence of a great religious service. The offering meant the Sioux felt sure of winning.

White Man Runs Him
Crow, a scout in Custer's cavalry unit

The scouts with General Custer were all Crows and Arikaras. Mitch Bouyer, a half-blood Sioux, was Chief of Scouts. The Crow scouts were Half Yellow Face, White Swan, Goes Ahead, Hairy Moccasin, Curly, and I, White Man Runs Him. I was one of the oldest of the scouts and did most of the advance scouting. I knew this country very well.

On June 24 we were camped at a place just below where Busby is now. Hairy Moccasin, Goes Ahead, and I took some soldiers' horses and rode to a high point on the divide between the Rosebud and the Little Horn. This place was used by the Crows as a lookout during campaigns, and from it you could see for miles around. In this hill was a pocket where horses could be hidden.

As soon as it became light enough to see, we could make out smoke from the Sioux camp down in the Little Horn Valley and could see some white horses on the other side of the Little Horn River. The soldiers had marched during the night and were now camped a little below us on Davis Creek. We could see the smoke of their campfires as they cooked breakfast. In a little while we saw the soldiers come marching up, and Custer stopped opposite to our lookout. I went down and told him about the smoke we had seen from the Sioux camp. This was about six o'clock in the morning.

Custer came up the hill far enough to see over and down the valley. When he saw the Sioux village, he said, "These people are very troublesome and bother the Crows and white people. I am going to teach them a lesson today. I will whip them, and you Crows may then live in peace."

We scouts thought there were too many Indians for Custer to fight. There were camps and camps and camps. One big camp was in a circle near the western hills. I would say there were between four thousand and five thousand warriors, maybe more, I do not know. It was the biggest Indian camp I have ever seen.

Black Elk
Oglala

I was thirteen years old the summer that Long Hair was rubbed out. We camped in the valley of the Greasy Grass. It was a very big village and you could hardly count the tepees. Farthest up the stream toward the south were the Hunkpapas, and the Oglalas were next. Then came the Miniconjous, the Sans Arcs, the Blackfeet, the Cheyennes; and last, the farthest toward the north, were the Santees and Yanktonais. Along the side toward the east was the Greasy Grass, with some timber along it, and it was running full from the melting of the snow in the Bighorn Mountains. If you stood on a hill, you could see the mountains off to the south and west. On the other side of the river, there were bluffs and hills beyond. Some gullies came down through the bluffs. On the westward side of us were lower hills, and there we grazed our ponies and guarded them. There were so many they could not be counted.

White Man Runs Him

We Crows made ready for battle. Goes Ahead tied some breath feathers into his braid. I painted sacred white clay stripes down my face. Half Yellow Face, who carried the pipe for the Crows, made a tobacco offering to the four winds. Seeing the little Crow ceremony, Custer came over.

"Why are you doing all this?" he asked.

With Mitch Bouyer interpreting, Half Yellow Face respectfully got to his feet and answered solemnly, "Because you and I are going home today, by a trail that is strange to all of us."

Custer moved forward, the soldiers going at a fast trot down Ash Creek. Our ponies were much smaller than the horses ridden by the soldiers, so we had to gallop most of the time to keep up.

Custer halted his command on a small flat about a mile and a quarter from the mouth of Ash Creek, and ordered Major Reno to swing out to the left, cross the Little Horn, and attack the upper end of the Sioux village. He saw some dust rising near the mouth of the creek and called Half Yellow Face, the leader of the Crows, over to him and asked what the dust was. Half Yellow Face said, "The Sioux must be running away." But Custer said, "I will throw my left wing south in case the Sioux should go that way." Then Reno moved out and crossed the creek just below the flat.

Custer then called White Swan and told him and Half Yellow Face to go over to the ridge and see what was going on in the Sioux camp. They started, but instead of going over to the ridge as they were told, they followed Reno, and that was the last we saw of them until the trouble was over. Then Custer started moving toward the ridge.

Young Hawk

Custer's orders to the Arikara scouts were this: "Go ahead riding hard, and capture as many Sioux horses as possible." Before the attack began, the older men spoke to the younger men, as is the custom of our tribe. Stabbed said, "Young men, keep up your courage. Don't behave like you are children. Today will be a hard battle." He said these things because he saw many of us were young and inexperienced. He wished to prepare us for our first real fight.

While Stabbed talked, he was rubbing some clay between his hands. Then he prayed: "My Father, I remember this day the promises you have made to me. It is for my young men I speak to you." Then he called up the young men and had us hold up our shirts in front so that he could rub the good medicine on our bodies. We came up one by one. He spit on the clay and then rubbed it on our chests. He had brought this clay with him from our home country for this purpose.

Every warrior then prepared himself for battle. I had a bunch of loose eagle feathers. I unbraided my hair, brought it forward on my head, and tied it with the eagle feathers. I expected to be killed and scalped by the Sioux, and I wanted to be ready to die.

Red Horse

Miniconjou

I was one of the chiefs of the council, and my lodge was pitched in the center of the camp. On the day of the attack, I and four women were out about a mile from camp digging wild turnips. Suddenly one of the women called my attention to a cloud of dust rising a short distance away. I soon saw that the soldiers were charging the camp.

We ran for the camp, and when I got there I was sent for at once to come to the council lodge. I found many of the council men already there when I arrived. We had no time to talk about what action we should take. We came out of the council lodge and called in all directions: Young men— mount horses and take guns; go fight the soldiers. Women and children—mount horses and go, get out of the way.

The day was hot. The soldiers came on the trail made by the Sioux camp in moving, and crossed the Little Bighorn River above where the Sioux crossed, and attacked the lodges of the Hunkpapas, farthest up the river.

Sitting Bull

I was lying in my lodge. Some young men ran in to me and said, "They are firing into the camp." I jumped up and stepped out of my lodge. The old men, the women, and the children were hurried away. There was great confusion. The women were like flying birds; the bullets were like humming bees. I said to the men: "Warriors, we have everything to fight for, and if we are defeated we shall have nothing to live for; therefore, let us fight like brave men."

Low Dog

I was asleep in my lodge at the time. The sun was about noon. I heard the alarm, but I did not believe it. I thought it was a false alarm. I did not think it possible that any white man would attack us, so strong as we were. We had in camp the Cheyennes, Arapahos, and seven different tribes of the Teton Sioux—a countless number.

Although I did not believe it was a true alarm, I lost no time getting ready. When I got my gun and came out of my lodge, the attack had begun at the end of the camp where Sitting Bull and the Hunkpapas were. The Indians held their ground to give the women and children time to get out of the way. By this time our herders were driving in our horses, and our men were catching them and hurrying to go and help those that were fighting.

When the fighters saw that the women and children were safe, they fell back. By this time my people were there to help them, and the older and less able warriors and the women caught horses and got them ready, and we drove the first attacking party back.

Iron Hawk
Hunkpapa

I am a Hunkpapa. I was fourteen years old the summer of the battle. The sun was overhead and more, but I was eating my first meal that day, because I had been sleeping. While I was eating, I heard the crier saying, "The chargers are coming!" I jumped up and rushed out to our horses. They were grazing close to camp. As I roped one, the others stampeded, but my older brother had caught his horse already and headed the others off. When I got on my horse with the rope hitched around his nose, the soldiers were shooting. I saw little children running up from the river where they had been swimming. All the women and children were running down the valley.

By now warriors were getting on the ponies and rushing toward the soldiers. Many of the warriors were already gathering in the brush and timber near the place where the soldiers had stopped and got off their horses. I rode past a very old man who was shouting, "Boys, take courage! Would you see these little children taken away from me like dogs?"

I went into our tepee and got dressed for war as fast as I

could, but I could hear bullets whizzing outside. I was so shaky that it took me a long time to braid an eagle feather into my hair. I also had to hold my pony's rope all the time, and he kept jerking me and trying to get away. While I was doing this, crowds of warriors on horses were roaring by upstream, yelling, "Hoka hey!" Then I rubbed red paint all over my face and took my bow and arrows and got on my horse. I did not have a gun, only a bow and arrows.

Black Elk

Out of the dust came the soldiers on their big horses. They looked big and strong and tall and they were all shooting. My brother took his gun and yelled for me to go back. There was brushy timber just on the other side of the Hunkpapas, and some warriors were gathering there. He made for that place, and I followed him. By now women and children were running in a crowd downstream. I looked back and saw them all running and scattering up a hillside down yonder.

When we got into the timber, a good many Hunkpapas were there already and the soldiers were shooting above us so that leaves were falling from the trees where the bullets struck. By now I could not see what was happening in the village below. It was all dust and cries and thunder, for the women and children were running there, and the warriors were coming on their ponies.

Among us there in the brush and out in the Hunkpapa camp a cry went up: "Take courage! Don't be a woman! The helpless are out of breath!" I think this was when Gall rallied the Hunkpapas, who had been running away, and turned them back.

Then another great cry went up out in the dust: "Crazy Horse is coming! Crazy Horse is coming!" Off toward the west and north they were making the tremolo and yelling, "Hoka hey!" like a big wind roaring. You could hear eagle-bone whistles screaming.

The valley went darker with dust and smoke, and there were only shadows and a big noise of many cries and hoofs and guns. On the left of where I was I could hear the shod hoofs of the soldiers' horses going back into the brush, and there was shooting everywhere. Then the hoofs came out of the brush, and I came out and was in among men and horses weaving in and out and going upstream, and everybody was yelling, "Hurry! Hurry!" The soldiers were running upstream, and we were all mixed there in the twilight and the great noise. I was small and could not crowd in to where the soldiers were, so I did not kill anybody. There were so many ahead of me, and it was all dark and mixed up.

Antelope Woman

In all the camps, as I went through them, there was great excitement. Old men were helping the young warriors in dressing and painting themselves for battle. Some women were bringing horses from the horse herd. Other women were working fast taking down their tepees. A few were loading horses with tepees and gear, while others were carrying heavy burdens on their backs. Many were taking away nothing, leaving their tepees and everything in them, running away with their children and only small packs in their hands. I saw a Sioux woman standing in one spot, jumping up and down screaming because she could not find her small son.

Wooden Leg

My brother and I ran to our camp and to our home lodge. I got my lariat and my six-shooter. I quickly emptied out my war bag and set myself at getting ready to go into battle. I jerked off my ordinary clothing. I jerked on a pair of new breeches that had been given to me by a Hunkpapa Sioux. I had a good cloth shirt, and I put it on. My old moccasins were kicked off and a pair of beaded moccasins substituted for them. My father had caught my favorite horse, and he strapped on a blanket and arranged the rawhide lariat into a bridle. He stood holding my mount.

"Hurry," he urged me.

I was hurrying, but I was not yet ready. I got my paints and my little mirror. The blue-black circle soon appeared around my face. The red and yellow colorings were applied on all of the skin inside the circle. I combed my hair. It properly should have been oiled and braided neatly, but my father again was saying, "Hurry," so I just looped a buckskin thong about it and tied it close up against the back of my head, to float loose from there.

A warrior preparing himself for battle presents his most

splendid personal appearance. That is, he gets himself ready to die. The idea of full dress in preparation for a battle does not come from a belief that it will add to the fighting ability. The preparation is for death, in case that should be the result of the conflict. Every Indian wants to look his best when he goes to meet the Great Spirit.

My bullets, caps, and powder horn put me into full readiness. In a moment I was on my horse, riding fast toward where all of the rest of the young men were going—out around and far beyond the Hunkpapa camp circle. Many hundreds of Indians on horseback were dashing to and fro in front of a body of soldiers. The soldiers were on the level valley ground and were shooting with rifles. Not many bullets were being sent back at them, but thousands of arrows were falling among them. I went on with a throng of Sioux until we got beyond and behind the white men. By this time, though, they had mounted their horses and were hiding themselves in the timber. A band of Indians were with the soldiers. It appeared they were Crows or Shoshones.

More and more of our people kept coming, and we extended our curved line farther and farther around the big grove of trees. Some dead soldiers had been left among the grass and sagebrush. It seemed to me the remainder of them would not live many hours longer. Sioux were creeping forward to set fire to the timber.

Suddenly the hidden soldiers came tearing out on horseback from the woods, running across an open space toward the river. We whipped our ponies into swift pursuit. The soldier horses moved slowly, as if they were very tired. Ours were lively. We gained rapidly on them.

I fired four shots with my six-shooter. I do not know whether or not any of my bullets did harm. Soldiers fell dead either from arrows or from stabbings or jabbings or from blows by the stone war clubs of the Sioux. Horses limped or staggered or sprawled out dead or dying. Our war cries and war songs were mingled with many jeering calls, such as: "You are only boys. You ought not to be fighting. We whipped you on the Rosebud. You should have brought more Crows or Shoshones with you to do your fighting."

Young Hawk

When the battle got stronger, the line curved back toward the river. Many of the soldiers were killed and they began to fall back. A swarm of Sioux forced the soldiers to begin to retreat back across the river.

Goose and I followed them and crossed the river where the water was deep and the sagebrush grew very thick on the opposite bank. The horses struggled hard before getting to land. We took refuge in a thick grove of trees. The Sioux were riding on all sides of us by this time. They began firing at us through the trees as we crouched there on horseback. I heard a sound like a sigh and Goose called to me, "Cousin, I am wounded." His right hand was badly shot.

I took off the cartridge belt belonging to Goose and put it on myself. I took off my army coat and shirt and got ready to fight for my life. I helped Goose to dismount just as his horse was shot down. I put him up against a tree and gave him the rope of my horse to hold. He had a revolver.

Just then I saw the Crow scout Half Yellow Face crawling toward me. He said, "My friend is being killed over in the thicket." We crawled on hands and knees back to where he lay on his back with his hands up. This was the Crow scout White Swan. We took him by his arms and dragged him back to where Goose sat by the tree.

White Swan said he was not afraid; he was proud to be wounded. The sight of these two wounded men stirred my heart. I did not want them to be mutilated by the enemy. I made up my mind I would die this day. I put my arms around the neck of my horse and said, "I love you." I then crawled out and stood up and saw all in front of me Sioux warriors kneeling ready to shoot. I fired at them and received a volley in return, but I was not hit. I was determined to try again to get killed, so I crawled out to the edge of the timber in a new place, jumped up and fired again. And again I received a volley, but I dropped out of sight before I was hit. Then I saw a nearby tree with driftwood piled against it, making very good protection. Behind it I found Forked Horn lying face down to avoid being shot.

When Forked Horn saw that it was me who had drawn the fire of the Sioux, he scolded me, saying, "Don't you do that again. To show yourself as a target is no way to fight." I sat still for a time after that, even while the Sioux tried to burn the scouts out. The grass was too green to catch on fire.

While this was going on, several Sioux women rode up and gave the high-pitched woman's yell urging the warriors to kill all the Arikaras. I heard them in many places about the bushes where I lay hiding, then they went away with the others. I had noticed that the Sioux attack was slackening. I saw them begin to ride off downstream. This was when Custer's attack had begun at the lower ford.

I stood up and looked around. On the ridge above me on the highest point I saw a United States flag. Forked Horn then said, "My grandson, you have shown yourself the bravest. The flag you have seen up there shows where the pack train is. We must now try to reach it."

With Goose and the wounded Crow, the scouts reached the surviving soldiers. The whole party retreated into a ravine nearby. Here the soldiers threw up breastworks, consisting of cracker boxes, bags of bacon, and other things from the packs.

The Sioux attacked us in this ravine, and the shooting made a continuous roar so that nothing else could be heard. This heavy firing went on without a break until it was dark.

Low Dog

I never before nor since saw men so brave and fearless as those white warriors. We retreated until our men all got together, and then we charged upon them. I called to my men, "This is a good day to die. Follow me!" We massed our men, and that no man should fall back, every man whipped another man's horse and rushed right upon them. As we rushed upon them, the white warriors dismounted to fire, but they did very poor shooting. They held their horses' reins on one arm while they were shooting, but their horses were so frightened that they pulled the men all around, and a great many of their shots went up in the air and did us no harm.

White Man Runs Him

Custer and his brother went to the right of us and halted on a small hill. His troops were moving forward below him. Custer turned around as he reached the top of the hill and waved his hat, and the soldiers at the bottom of the hill waved their hats and shouted. Custer then proceeded on up the ridge and his men followed. They were moving rapidly, and the scouts were forced to gallop their ponies sometimes to keep up with them. At a certain point on the ridge they turned to the right and rode down a coulee in a northern direction.

The scouts took up a position on the high bluffs, where we could look down into the Sioux camp. As we followed along on the high ground, Custer had come down Medicine Tail Creek and was moving toward the river. The Indians saw him there, and all began running that way. There were thousands of them. Custer tried to cross the river at the mouth of Medicine Tail Creek, but was unable to do so. This was the last we saw Custer.

Mitch Bouyer said to us, "You scouts need go no farther. You have guided Custer here, and your work is finished, so you had better go back to the pack train and let the soldiers do the fighting." Mitch Bouyer said that he was going down to join Custer, and turning his horse, he galloped away. That is the last time we saw Mitch Bouyer. He was killed with Custer over on the ridge.

Red Horse

The soldiers stopped on a hill, and the Sioux surrounded them. A Sioux man came and said that a different party of soldiers had all the women and children prisoners. Like a whirlwind, the word went around, and the Sioux all heard it and left the soldiers on the hill and went quickly to save the women and children.

The attack was made on the Sioux camp about noon. The soldiers, it appears, were divided, one party charging right into the camp. We drove them across the creek. When we attacked the other party, we swarmed down on them and drove them in confusion. Some soldiers became panic-stricken, throwing down their guns and raising up their hands, saying, "Sioux, pity us; take us prisoners." The Sioux did not take a single soldier prisoner, but killed all of them. None were left alive even for a few minutes.

The second party of soldiers made five brave stands. Once we charged right in until we scattered them all, fighting among them hand to hand. One band of soldiers was behind the Sioux. When they charged, we fell back and stood for one moment facing each other. Then all the Sioux got courage

and started for them in a solid body. We went only a little distance before we spread out and encircled them. All the time
I could see their officers riding in front and hear them shouting to their men. It was in this charge that most of the Sioux
were killed. We finished up this party right there in the
ravine.

From the place of the second fight to the hill that the first
soldiers were on was level ground with the exception of a
creek. We thought the soldiers on the hill would charge us
from the rear. When they did not, we thought the soldiers on
the hill were out of cartridges. As soon as we had killed all the
second party, the Sioux all went back to kill the soldiers on
the hill. Had the soldiers not divided, I think they would have
killed many Sioux.

Two Moon
Cheyenne

After watching the fight near the Hunkpapa circle, I returned to my camp. I thought the danger was past, and I stopped the women from carrying off the lodges. While I was sitting on my horse, I saw flags come up over the hill to the east. Then the soldiers rose all at once. A bugle sounded and they all got off their horses and some soldiers led the horses back over the hill.

Then the Sioux rode up the ridge on all sides, riding very fast. The Cheyennes went up the left way. The shooting was quick: *pop—pop—pop*—very fast. Some of the soldiers were down on their knees, some standing. The officers were all in front. The smoke was like a great cloud, and everywhere the Sioux went the dust rose like smoke. We circled all round them—swirling like water round a stone. We shoot, we ride fast, we shoot again. Soldiers dropped, and horses fell on them. The soldiers in line dropped, but one man rode up and down the line—all the time shouting. He rode a sorrel horse with a white face and white forelegs. I don't know who he was. He was the bravest man.

Standing Bear

Miniconjou

We went downstream to the mouth of Muskrat Creek beyond the Santee camp. There were warriors ahead of us, the "fronters," who are the bravest and have had most practice in war. I was sixteen years old, and I was in the rear with the less brave. When we got farther up the hill, I could see the soldiers. They were off their horses, holding them by the bridles. They were ready for us and were shooting. Our people were all around the hill on every side by this time. I heard some of our men shouting, "They are gone!" And I saw that many of the soldiers' horses had broken loose and were running away. Everywhere our warriors began yelling, "Hoka hey! Hurry! Hurry!"

Then we all went up, and it got dark with dust and smoke. I could see warriors flying all around me like shadows, and the noise of all those hoofs and guns and cries was so loud it seemed quiet in there and the voices seemed to be on top of the cloud. It was like a bad dream. All at once I saw a soldier right beside me, and I leaned over and knocked him down with the butt of the six-shooter. I think I had already shot it empty, but I don't remember when. The soldier fell off and was under the hoofs. There were so many of us that I think we did not need guns. Just the hoofs would have been enough.

After this we started down the hillside toward the village, and there were dead men and horses scattered along there too. They were all rubbed out.

Antelope Woman

"Let me have a horse," I begged my brother White Bull. I had seen other battles in the past. I always liked to watch; not many women did that, and I had often been teased about it. But this time I had a good excuse, for White Bull's son, my nephew named Noisy Walking, was gone. I was then twenty-nine years old, and as I did not have any son to serve as a warrior, I could sing strongheart songs for my nephew. He was eighteen years old. Some women told me he expected me to be there, and he had wrapped a red scarf around his neck so that I could see him at a distance.

I rode far to the right, keeping all the time out of the range of the bullets. I looked and looked for Noisy Walking. Although I was singing strongheart songs, thinking he might hear me, I had not seen him.

My heart thumped loud as I saw an Indian leading a horse bearing a rider who appeared to be wounded. The rider resembled my nephew. I whipped up my horse and caught up with the two men. But they were both Sioux, so I went back to the fight.

A few women besides me were watching the battle. We

were not there to do any fighting, but we were just looking and cheering our men with our songs. All of us had sheath knives, and some of us had hatchets. But these were carried in our belts all the time for use in our work, not for hurting people. Most of the women who watched the battle stayed out of the reach of bullets, as I did. But there was one who stayed close in at all times: she was Calf Trail Woman. She had a pistol with bullets, and she fired many shots at the soldiers. She was the only woman there who had a gun. She kept on her horse all the time, but she kept close to her husband, Black Coyote, who was one of the Indians creeping close to the ridges, up the gulches. At one time she was about to give her pony to a young Cheyenne who had lost his own, but I called out to them, "Our women have plenty of good horses for you down by the river." I was speaking of the soldier horses that had run away down there and had been caught by our people. She took the young Cheyenne up behind her on her pony, and they rode down to the river.

Wooden Leg

Bows and arrows were in use much more than guns. An Indian using a gun had to jump up and expose himself long enough to shoot. From their hiding places, Indians could shoot arrows in a high and long curve, to fall upon the soldiers or their horses. The arrows falling upon the horses stuck in their backs and caused them to go plunging here and there, knocking down the soldiers. The ponies of our warriors who were creeping along the gulches had been left farther back. Some of them were let loose, dragging their ropes, but most of them were tied to sagebrush. The Indians all the time could see where the soldiers were on the ridge, but the soldiers could not see our warriors crawling in the gullies through the sagebrush.

After this time of slow fighting, about forty of the soldiers came galloping from the east part of the ridge down toward the river, toward where most of the Cheyennes and many Oglalas were hidden. The Indians ran back to a deep gulch. The soldiers stopped and got off their horses when they arrived at a low ridge where the Indians had been. Lame White Man, the Southern Cheyenne chief, came on his horse and called us to come back and fight. In a few minutes the warriors were all around these soldiers. Then Lame White Man called out: "Come. We can kill all of them."

All around, the Indians began jumping up, running forward, dodging down, jumping up again, down again, all the time going toward the soldiers. Right away, all of the white men went crazy. Instead of shooting us, they turned their guns upon themselves. Almost before we could get to them, every one of them was dead. They killed themselves.

The Indians took the guns of these soldiers and used them for shooting at the soldiers on the high ridge. The shots quit coming from the soldiers. Warriors who had crept close to them began to call out that all of the white men were dead. All of the Indians then jumped up and rushed forward. All of the boys and old men on their horses came tearing into the crowd. The air was full of dust and smoke. Everybody was greatly excited. It looked like thousands of dogs might look if all of them were mixed together in a fight.

A strange incident happened: It appeared that all of the white men were dead. But there was one of them who raised himself to a support on his left elbow. He turned and looked over his left shoulder, and then I got a good view of him. His expression was wild, as if his mind was all tangled up and he was wondering what was going on here. In his right hand he held his six-shooter. Many of the Indians near him were scared by what seemed to have been a return from death to life. But a Sioux warrior jumped forward, grabbed the six-shooter, and wrenched it from the soldier's grasp. The gun was turned upon the white man, and he was shot through the head. Other Indians struck him or stabbed him. I think he must have been the last man killed in this great battle where not one of the enemy got away.

Noisy Walking was badly wounded. He was my same age, and we often had been companions since our small boyhood. White Bull, an important medicine man, was his father. I asked the young man, "How are you?" He replied, "Good." But he did not look well. He had been hit by three different bullets, one of them having passed through his body. He had also some stab wounds in his side. Word had been sent to his relatives in the camp.

Sitting Bull

I tell no lies about dead men. These men who came with Long Hair were as good men as ever fought. When they rode up, their horses were tired and they were tired. When they got off from their horses, they could not stand firmly on their feet. They swayed to and fro—so my young men have told me—like the limbs of cypresses in a great wind. Some of them staggered under the weight of their guns. But they began to fight at once; but by this time, as I have said, our camps were aroused, and there were plenty of warriors to meet them. They fired with needle guns. We replied with magazine guns—repeating rifles. Our young men rained lead across the river and drove the white braves back.

Antelope Woman

I went riding among the different Indians on the battlefield in search of Noisy Walking. A Cheyenne told me where my nephew was, down in a deep gulch halfway to the river. I went there and found him. He had been shot through the body and had been stabbed several times. I stayed with him while a young warrior friend went to the camp to tell his mother.

Women from the camps brought lodge-pole travois, dragged by ponies, to take away the dead and wounded Indians. Noisy Walking's mother and sister came to get him. We put him on a travois and took him across the river to the camp.

Wooden Leg

I helped in putting my friend Noisy Walking on the travois when his father and mother and women relatives came after him. Judging by his appearance then, this was the last good act I ever should do for him. Various groups of women, many more of the Sioux than of the Cheyennes, were on the field searching for and taking away their dead and wounded men. I did not like to hear the weeping of the women. My heart that had been glad because of the victory was made sad by thoughts of our own dead and dying men and their mourning relatives left behind.

Black Elk

I watched the big dust whirling on the hill across the river, and horses were coming out of it with empty saddles. We knew there would be no soldiers left. There were many other boys about my age and younger up there with their mothers and sisters, and they asked me to go over to the battle with them. So we got on our ponies and rode over across the Greasy Grass to the mouth of a gulch that led up through the bluff to where the fighting was. We rode around shooting arrows into the soldiers.

I saw something bright hanging on this soldier's belt, and I pulled it out. It was round and bright and yellow and very beautiful and I put it on for a necklace. At first it ticked inside, and then it did not anymore. I wore it around my neck a long time before I found out what it was and how to make it tick again.

Then the women all came over and we went to the top of the hill. Gray horses were lying dead there, and some of them were on top of dead soldiers, and dead soldiers were on top of them. After a while I got tired looking around. I could smell nothing but blood, and I got sick of it. So I went back home with some others. I was not sorry at all. I was a happy boy. Those white soldiers had come to kill our mothers and fathers and us, and it was our country.

Wooden Leg

I took a folded leather package from a soldier having three stripes on the left arm of his coat. It had in it lots of flat pieces of green paper having pictures or writing I did not then understand. I tore it all up and gave the leather holder to a Cheyenne friend. Others got packages of the same kind from other dead white men. Some of it was kept by the finders. But most of it was thrown away or was given to boys, for them to look at the pictures.

I had on a soldier coat and breeches I had taken. I rode among our people. The first person I met who took special interest in me was my mother's mother. She was living in a little willow dome lodge of her own. I told her about my having killed the Crow or Shoshone at the first fight up the river, about my getting the two guns, about my knocking in the head two soldiers in the river, about what I had done in the next fight on the hill where all of the soldiers had been killed. We talked about my soldier clothing. Neither the coat nor the breeches fit me well. The arms and legs were too short for me. But she said I looked good dressed that way. I had thought so too.

Sitting Bull

I warned my people not to touch the spoils of the battlefield, not to take the guns and horses from the dead soldiers. Many did not heed, and it will prove a curse to this nation. Indians who set their hearts upon the goods of the white man will be at his mercy and will starve at his hands.

Wooden Leg

After sundown I visited Noisy Walking. He was lying on a ground bed of buffalo robes under a willow dome shelter. His father, White Bull, was with him. His mother sat just outside the entrance. I asked my friend, "How are you?" He replied, "Good, only I want water." I did not know what else to say, but I wanted him to know that I was his friend and willing to do whatever I could for him. I sat down upon the ground beside him. After a little while I said, "You were brave." Nothing else was said for several minutes. He was weak. His hands trembled at every move he made. Finally he said to his father, "I wish I could have some water—just a little of it."

"No. Water will kill you."

White Bull almost choked as he said this to his son. But he was a good medicine man, and he knew what was best. As I sat there looking at Noisy Walking, I knew he was going to die. My heart was heavy. But I could not do him any good, so I excused myself and went away.

Low Dog

The next day we fought Reno and his forces again and killed many of them. Then the chiefs said these men had been punished enough, and that we ought to be merciful and let them go. Then we heard that another force was coming up the river; this was General Terry's command. The chiefs and wise men counseled that we had fought enough and that we should not fight unless attacked. So we took our women and children and went away.

Black Elk

About sundown of the second day our scouts had reported that more soldiers were coming upstream; so we all broke camp. Before dark we were ready and we started up the Greasy Grass, heading for the Bighorn Mountains. We fled all night, following the Greasy Grass. My two younger brothers and I rode in a pony-drag, and my mother put some young puppies in with us. They were always trying to crawl out and I was always putting them back in, so I didn't sleep much.

By morning we reached a little dry creek and made camp and had a big feast. The meat had spots of fat in it, and I wish I had some of it right now.

When it was full day, we started again and came to Wood Louse Creek at the foot of the mountains, and camped there. The scouts reported that the soldiers had not followed us and that everything was safe now. All over the camp there were big fires and Kill Dances all night long.

Red Horse

Among the soldiers was an officer who rode a horse with four white feet. The Sioux have for a long time fought many brave men of different peoples, but the Sioux say this officer was the bravest man they had ever fought. I don't know whether this was General Custer or not. Many of the Sioux men that I hear talking tell me it was. I saw this officer in the fight many times, but did not see his body. It has been told me that he was killed by a Santee Indian, who took his horse. This officer wore a large-brimmed hat and buckskin coat. This officer saved the lives of many soldiers by turning his horse and covering the retreat.

There are many little incidents connected with this fight, but I don't recollect them now. I don't like to talk about that fight. If I hear any of my people talking about it, I always move away.

Antelope Woman

I may have seen Custer at the time of the battle or after he was killed. I do not know. At the time I did not know he was there. All of our old warriors say the same—none of them knew of his being there till they were told of it at the soldier fort or at the agencies or heard it from Indians coming from the agencies. But I learned something more about him later from our people in Oklahoma. Two Southern Cheyenne women who had known him in the south had seen Custer lying dead on the battlefield after the fight ended. They pushed the point of a bone sewing awl through his ears. They did this to improve his hearing in the spirit world. He must not have listened very well in this life, or he would have heard what our chiefs said about broken promises.

Epilogue

The morning after Custer's destruction, hundreds of warriors, many of them now armed with rifles and pistols taken from dead soldiers, returned to attack the troopers still huddled with Reno and Benteen on the bluffs to the south of the village. The Indians kept up a terrific fire on the trapped soldiers until Sitting Bull sent word to stop the fighting. "Let them go," Sitting Bull declared. "Let them live. They have come against us, and we have killed a few. If we kill them all, they will send a bigger army against us."

About this time, word arrived that the soldiers with Terry and Gibbon were approaching. Because everyone was tired of fighting, the chiefs decided to move camp to a place of safety, where the wounded could rest and the victory be celebrated. The women immediately began taking down the tepees and packing their belongings. By noon the huge camp was on the march. Like a giant snake it wound across the open prairie toward the Bighorn Mountains, several days' march away. In their wake, the Indians left a blazing prairie fire. The fire was set to burn the grass and deprive cavalry horses of forage, should the army choose to follow, and to signal to all Indians in the area that Sitting Bull had earned a great victory.

It had indeed been a great victory. Altogether the Indians killed 263 men, including three Arikara scouts: 212 with Custer and 51 with Reno. The Indians suffered far fewer casualties. Only thirty or so warriors had been killed, although many more had been wounded. Several women and children had also died in the initial attack on the village. Some of the Indians who died were "suicide" warriors who had vowed beforehand to be killed in battle. A few Indians had been killed accidentally or wounded in the crossfire because the

The site of Custer's defeat, photographed a year later, in 1877: horse bones and an "Unknown" grave marker.

thick dust and smoke made it impossible sometimes to tell friend from foe.

For the Lakota and their Cheyenne allies, however, the victory over Custer would be their undoing. The disaster on the Little Bighorn shocked and embarrassed the U.S. Army. As a result, the military pursued Crazy Horse and Sitting Bull and their followers with relentless vengeance. Even in the dead of winter, when the Plains Indians normally went into camp and waited patiently for spring, they got no rest. Between July 1876 and May 1877, Crook's forces and a newly arrived unit under General Nelson Miles defeated Dull Knife,

"Custer's Last Fight," by William de la Moutagne Cary, published in 1876.

Crazy Horse, Lame Deer, and other chiefs who had taken part in the Battle of the Little Bighorn. In May 1877, Crazy Horse led his band into the Red Cloud Agency in South Dakota and surrendered. Four months later, he was stabbed to death under mysterious circumstances while supposedly resisting arrest. "It is good," remarked one of his saddened followers. "Crazy Horse has looked for death and it has come."

Sitting Bull managed to elude capture for a time. As the army continued its relentless search for the Indian bands that had participated in the Custer fight, Sitting Bull, Gall, and several hundred followers crossed the border into Canada, where they remained safe. But life was lonely and hard in Canada, where there were few buffalo to hunt. In small groups, the refugees quietly began returning to their friends and relatives until the remaining diehards, fewer than fifty families loyal to Sitting Bull, surrendered with him in 1881.

For the next two years Sitting Bull was a virtual prisoner of the U.S. government, but he enjoyed great notoriety for his role in defeating Custer. One of those to capitalize on his renown was William F. Cody, better known as Buffalo Bill. Cody, who operated a successful "Wild West show" that toured cities in the United States and abroad, got permission

Lakota prisoners of the U.S. Army holding a Seventh Cavalry flag captured at the Battle of the Little Bighorn.

from the Bureau of Indian Affairs to let Sitting Bull tour with him for one season in 1885.

Although now an old man, Sitting Bull was still feared and mistrusted by government officials. Their suspicions appeared confirmed when he became an advocate of the Ghost Dance religion that was adopted by Indians across the West in the late 1880s.

Defeated, dispirited, and trapped on their barren reservations, many western Indians sought escape through the Ghost Dance religion. Led by an Indian prophet named Wovoka, who urged his followers to return to the Indian way of life, the

Ghost Dancers were convinced that all whites would disappear, all dead Indians would return to life, and the buffalo would return to the plains in vast numbers.

Within a remarkably short time, large numbers of tribespeople on the Lakota reservations in North and South Dakota embraced the new religion, which was regarded by government officials as militaristic and anti-white. When Sitting Bull threatened to join the Dancers, government officials decided to have him arrested. The result was a fierce gun battle on December 15, 1890, in which the old chief, seven of his followers, and six Indian policemen died.

The Ghost Dance phenomenon ended two weeks later,

White Man Runs Him,
a Crow warrior.

Two Moon, a Cheyenne leader.

on December 29, 1890, at
Wounded Knee, when the
Seventh Cavalry—Custer's
former regiment—tried to
disarm a Miniconjou band of
Ghost Dancers led by Chief
Big Foot. The result was a
massacre, in which some
three hundred frightened,
freezing men, women, and
children died. Wounded Knee
is often said to mark the end

Gall, the Hunkpapa leader.

of the Indian wars on the northern plains, but in reality
the wars had ended within months of Sitting Bull's stun-
ning victory on the banks of the Greasy Grass.

Perhaps the cruelest fate befell the Northern Cheyennes.
While in camp the winter after the battle, they were attacked
by cavalrymen and driven from their homes into the snow.
The soldiers then destroyed their tepees, clothing, and food
supply. That night eleven Cheyenne babies froze to death.
When spring came, the Northern Cheyennes surrendered.

Although the Cheyennes expected to be placed on a reservation, they did not anticipate being relocated to Indian Territory in present-day Oklahoma, more than a thousand miles from their homeland on the northern plains. It was their misfortune to become part of a new government program to concentrate as many tribes as possible in a relatively small region. Eventually some twenty-five tribes were moved to Indian Territory, which explains why so many tribes live in Oklahoma today.

The Northern Cheyennes hated Oklahoma. "In Oklahoma we all got sick with chills and fever," recalled Iron Teeth, an elderly Cheyenne woman who told her story in 1927. "When we were not sick, we were hungry."

In September 1877, some three hundred Northern Cheyennes under Chiefs Dull Knife and Little Wolf decided to go home. Despite the fact that only one in five was a warrior and that they had few weapons and horses and little food, the refugees managed to elude the thousands of troops attempting to intercept them. Upon reaching the Dakota country, the Cheyennes split into two groups. Some chose to follow Little Wolf, who spent the winter deep in the Wyoming wilderness; the others surrendered with Dull Knife at Fort Robinson, Nebraska—only to be told that they would have to return to Oklahoma. When they refused, the Cheyennes were locked in unheated barracks without food or water. During the night of January 9, 1878, the prisoners made a suicidal break for freedom. Of 149 held in the barracks, 64 were killed. Most of the others, many gravely wounded, were recaptured.

Iron Teeth's experiences were probably typical. Her husband had died in an attack on their village. With her five children she went to Oklahoma and then participated in the escape. When the group separated, a son and daughter went with Little Wolf. She and her remaining children, including a twenty-two-year-old son named Gathering His Medicine,

Iron Teeth, photographed in 1927.

followed Dull Knife to Fort Robinson. During the breakout, Iron Teeth kept one daughter with her, and they were found hiding in a cave the following day. Her son, who had a pistol, carried the youngest girl on his back into another cave. When soldiers tracking him through the snow reached the cave, Gathering His Medicine told his sister to stay hidden while he went outside to challenge them. "Lots of times," Iron Teeth said, "as I sit here alone on the floor with my blanket wrapped about me, I lean forward and close my eyes and think of him...fighting the soldiers, knowing that he would be killed, but doing this so his little sister might get away in safety. Don't you think he was a brave young man?"

Today the Custer battlefield is a national park. Each year it is visited by thousands of people from all over the world. Only

Wooden Leg, photographed in 1927 during an interview with Thomas Marquis, a doctor who collected Indian accounts of the Battle of the Little Bighorn.

in recent years, however, have Indians begun visiting the battlefield. "The reason for this is easy to explain," says Gerard Baker, the superintendent of the battlefield, who is himself related to the Arikara scouts who were with Custer. "The battle represents the end of the way of life for Indian people. When Indians visit the battlefield today, some cry. Many get angry. They are upset for the loss of that way of life, that freedom we once enjoyed. It's something we Indian people will never get back. That is what the battlefield means to us."

Biographical Notes

ANTELOPE WOMAN, Northern Cheyenne, was the sister of White Bull, whose son Noisy Walking was killed in the battle. In later life, Antelope Woman was known as Kate Big Head. She told her story of the Battle of the Little Bighorn to Thomas Marquis, who published it as *She Watched Custer's Last Battle* in 1933.

BLACK ELK, Oglala, was born in 1863 along the Little Powder River in northeast Wyoming. He was only thirteen years old at the time of the Custer fight. A distant cousin of Crazy Horse, he had a long and fascinating life. He went to Canada with Sitting Bull and later toured with Buffalo Bill's Wild West Show. Black Elk became a person of great spiritual power and later told his story to poet John Neihardt, who published it in 1932 as *Black Elk Speaks: The Life Story of a Holy Man of the Oglala Sioux*. He died in 1950.

CRAZY HORSE, an Oglala chief, was born near Bear Butte, in what is now South Dakota, in about 1840. One of the most inspirational leaders of the Lakota, he was so fiercely independent that he refused to allow his photograph to be taken or his portrait painted and, like Sitting Bull, refused to sign a treaty or have any dealings with the federal government. However, he surrendered in May 1877, a year after the battle with Custer, and was later killed by soldiers while resisting an attempt to put him in a jail cell.

GALL, Hunkpapa, was born in 1840 in present-day South Dakota. He was adamantly opposed to reservation life and, like Sitting Bull, fled to Canada with his band after the battle. In the winter of 1880 he surrendered to U.S. authorities and then became a progressive leader of his people as a reservation Indian, serving as a justice of the Indian Police Court on Standing Rock Reservation. He died in 1893.

IRON HAWK, Hunkpapa, was born in 1862 in what is now Montana. In 1907 he told his story to several historians.

LOW DOG, an Oglala chief, was a respected warrior.

RED HORSE was a Miniconjou chief. His band surrendered at the Cheyenne River Indian Agency in 1877. In 1881 he made a series of pencil drawings that described the Battle of the Little Bighorn. These drawings are now in the Smithsonian Institution.

SITTING BULL, Hunkpapa. Born in present-day South Dakota about 1831, he was a member of the Strong Heart Society and spiritual leader of the Hunkpapa Lakota. After the Battle of the Little Bighorn, he and his immediate followers fled to Canada, where they remained about five years. Upon his return, Buffalo Bill persuaded Sitting Bull to tour with his Wild West Show for a year. Sitting Bull then retired to the Standing Rock Reservation, where he was killed on December 15, 1890, while resisting arrest during the Ghost Dance hysteria.

STANDING BEAR, Miniconjou, was born on the Tongue River in present-day Montana, in 1859. He gave several interviews about the Custer fight in his old age, including one to John Neihardt in 1931.

TWO MOON. A Cheyenne leader, Two Moon was born in what is now western Wyoming in 1842 and died on the Northern Cheyenne Reservation in Montana in 1917.

WHITE MAN RUNS HIM, Crow, was one of the six Crow scouts at the Battle of the Little Bighorn. He was born around 1858 near the town of Edgar, in what is now Montana. He died on the Crow Reservation in 1929. At the time of the Custer fight, he was probably eighteen years old.

WOODEN LEG, Northern Cheyenne, was born in 1858 along the Cheyenne River in what is now South Dakota. In his later life he served as a scout for the U.S. Army. He told the story of his life to Thomas Marquis, who then published it as an autobiography in 1931 under the title *A Warrior Who Fought Custer*. Wooden Leg died on the Northern Cheyenne Reservation in 1940.

YOUNG HAWK was an Arikara scout. At the time of the Custer fight, he was seventeen years old.

Chronology

1851 First Treaty of Fort Laramie between the U.S. government and the Indians of the northern Great Plains defines territories belonging to the Lakota and other Indian tribes.

1854–55 Conflict between Indians and settlers traveling along the Oregon Trail leads to the "Grattan Affair": A Lakota band led by Conquering Bear, and including the young Crazy Horse, wipes out a U.S. Army detachment led by Lieutenant John Grattan. In response, the U.S. Army attacks a Lakota village at Blue Water, killing 85.

1862 Homestead Act makes land in the Nebraska and Kansas Territories available to settlers who farm claims continuously for five years.

1862 Lakota living along the Minnesota River respond to white trespasses on their lands with raids on white settlements, trading posts, and forts. Under the leadership of Little Crow, they at first inflict heavy losses on the U.S. Army but are eventually defeated. In *December 1862*, 38 Lakota participants in the uprising are hanged in the largest mass execution in U.S. history.

1863 John Bozeman establishes a direct route to the gold fields of Montana and the West, known as the Bozeman Trail, through Indian lands west of the Black Hills.

1866–68 Red Cloud's War. Lakota, Cheyenne, and Arapaho Indians led by Red Cloud, Crazy Horse, Dull Knife, and others repeatedly defeat U.S. Army units attempting to establish forts along the Bozeman Trail.

1868 Second Treaty of Fort Laramie ends U.S. attempts to fortify the Bozeman Trail. Treaty creates the Great Sioux Reservation west of the Missouri River in present-day South Dakota.

1869 First transcontinental railroad completed. Around this time, surveys also begin for a new railroad, the Northern Pacific, passing through Indian territory.

1874 Expedition led by Lieutenant Colonel George

Armstrong Custer discovers gold in the Black Hills, leading to a flood of prospectors entering land sacred to the Lakota and Cheyenne.

1875–76 U.S. Army under the command of William Tecumseh Sherman attempts to force nomadic Lakota bands led by Sitting Bull and Crazy Horse out of the Black Hills and onto the Great Lakota Reservation. Crazy Horse defeats army units at Powder River in *March 1876* and Rosebud Creek in *June 1876*.

June 25, 1876 Battle of the Little Bighorn. Lakota and Cheyenne warriors led by Sitting Bull, Crazy Horse, Gall, and others defeat U.S. Seventh Cavalry under Custer. A total of 263 soldiers are killed, including Custer and his entire detachment of 212.

July 1876–May 1877 U.S. Army defeats Lakota and Cheyenne bands in a succession of battles. Sitting Bull takes refuge in Canada. The Cheyenne leader Dull Knife surrenders in *May 1877*. In *September 1877*, Crazy Horse is killed while resisting arrest.

1881   Sitting Bull returns to U.S. and surrenders at Fort Buford, Dakota Territory.

1890   Ghost Dance religion spreads among Lakota Indians living on reservations in South Dakota. On *December 15, 1890*, Sitting Bull is killed while attempting to leave the Standing Rock Reservation. On *December 29, 1890*, some 300 Lakota are killed by U.S. Army troops at Wounded Knee Creek in South Dakota.

A Note on Sources

Almost immediately after the Battle of the Little Bighorn, investigators eagerly sought information about what had happened to Custer and the troopers under his command. Since no one with Custer survived, the details of the battle would have to come from the victorious Indians—but they were in full-scale retreat from vengeful U.S. Army units seeking to punish them and put them on reservations. Many years passed before the Indian side of the story began to be told. Even then, many Indians present that day in 1876 were fearful of telling what they knew. They thought the government would arrest them and put them in jail or even execute them. By then Custer had become an American legend, and no one wished to believe he had behaved improperly or recklessly. Most of the Indian veterans of the battle knew this, so they were especially cautious about saying anything that would anger the government, relatives of the slain soldiers, or the U.S. Army. As a result, much valuable information was lost to history.

However, some white historians who befriended certain Indian veterans were able to collect their stories about the

Custer fight. It is those stories that made this book possible. One of the most important historians was an obscure but dedicated doctor who for many years worked with the Cheyenne and Crow people on their reservations in Montana. Fascinated by the Custer fight, Dr. Thomas Marquis sought out and befriended elderly Lakota, Cheyenne, and Crow veterans of the battle. Most of these aged Indians could not speak English, so Dr. Marquis became expert in using sign language. The old Indians liked their kind white friend who gave them food, money, and medical care. The Indians spoke honestly and freely with him even though they would have nothing to do with other white people.

By the time he died in 1935, Dr. Marquis had published many books and articles about the Indian side of the Custer fight. His most important books are *Keep the Last Bullet for Yourself, Memoirs of a White Crow Indian,* and *Wooden Leg: A Warrior Who Fought Custer.*

Sources of material used in this book are:

W. A. Graham, *The Custer Myth: A Source Book of Custeriana.* Stackpole Books, reprint edition, 1995.

Richard G. Hardoff, *Lakota Recollections of the Custer Fight:*

New Sources of Indian-Military History. University of Nebraska Press, 1997.

O. G. Libby, *The Arikara Narrative of the Campaign Against the Hostile Dakotas*. North Dakota Historical Commission, 1920.

Thomas B. Marquis, *She Watched Custer's Last Battle*. Privately printed, 1933.

Thomas B. Marquis, *Wooden Leg: A Warrior Who Fought Custer*. University of Nebraska Press, reprint edition, 1962.

David Humphreys Miller, *Custer's Fall: The Native American Side of the Story*. Meridian, reprint edition, 1992.

Index

Iron Hawk, 36-37, 86
Iron Teeth, 80-82

Lakota peoples, viii, 1-3
   Army revenge on, 75-76
   hunting grounds, 6, 19, 25
   and Little Bighorn, 11-16
   mutual protection, 9, 21
   and Rosebud Creek, 9-10
   tribes of, 11
   vs. white settlers, 5, 7-8
Lame Deer, Chief, 76
Lame White Man, Chief, 10, 57-58
Little Bighorn, Battle of, 1, 11-16
   action, 44-59
   after the battle, 68-71, 74, 79
   chronology, 89-92
   end of the battle, 60-67
   epilogue, 73-83
   first attack, 33-43
   map, 13
   preparation, 27-32, 41-42

Little Wolf, Chief, 80-81
Long Hair, *see* Custer, Col. George A.
Low Dog, 20, 35, 47, 68, 86

Marquis, Thomas, 82
Miles, Gen. Nelson, 75
Miniconjou tribe, 11, 21, 29, 33, 53-54, 79

Noisy Walking, 55, 59, 61, 62, 67

Oglala tribe, 5, 11, 20, 21, 29, 57

Red Cloud, 5, 6
Red Horse, 33, 50-51, 70, 86-87
Reno, Maj. Marcus, 12-15, 30, 31, 68, 73
reservations, 5-9, 20, 80-81
Rosebud Creek, Battle of, 8-10, 23, 24

Photographic Credits

Pages 5, 10, 74, 77, 78 *left*, 79, 81, 82: The Smithsonian Institution. Page 6 *top*: National Museum of the American Indian, Smithsonian Institution. Page 6 *bottom*: Glen Swanson Collection. Page 8: Burlington Northern Railroad Archives. Page 14: Little Bighorn Battlefield National Monument. Page 15: Yale Collection of Western Americana, Beinecke Rare Book and Manuscript Library. Page 75: Library of Congress. Page 78 *right*: Panhandle-Plains Historical Museum Research Center, Canyon, Texas.